The
COMPANIONS *in Christ*
Network

www.companionsinchrist.org

So much more!

Companions in Christ is *so much more* than printed resources.
It offers an ongoing LEADERSHIP NETWORK that provides:

- ➤ Opportunities to connect with other small groups who are also journeying through the *Companions in Christ* series.
- ➤ Insights and testimonies from other *Companions in Christ* participants
- ➤ An online discussion room where you can share or gather information
- ➤ Training opportunities that develop and deepen the leadership skills used in formational groups
- ➤ Helpful leadership tips and articles as well as updated lists of supplemental resources

Just complete this form and drop it in the mail, and you can enjoy the many benefits available through the *Companions in Christ* NETWORK! Or, enter your contact information at www.companionsinchrist.org/leaders.

Name: _____

Address: _____

City/State/Zip: _____

Church: _____

Email: _____

Phone: _____

COMPANIONS *in Christ*
Upper Room Ministries
PO Box 340012
Nashville, TN 37203-9540

COMPANIONS *in Christ*
A SMALL-GROUP EXPERIENCE IN SPIRITUAL FORMATION

EMBRACING
~ *the* JOURNEY

Participant's Book | Volume 1

Rueben P. Job | Marjorie J. Thompson

UPPER ROOM BOOKS®
NASHVILLE

COMPANIONS IN CHRIST
EMBRACING THE JOURNEY: THE WAY OF CHRIST
Participant's Book: Part 1
Copyright © 2006 by Upper Room Books®
All rights reserved.

The Upper Room® Web site http://www.upperroom.org

UPPER ROOM®, UPPER ROOM BOOKS® and design logos are trademarks owned by the Upper Room®, a ministry of GBOD®, Nashville, Tennessee. All rights reserved.

At the time of publication all Web sites referenced in this book were valid. However, due to the fluid nature of the Internet some addresses may have changed or the content may no longer be relevant.

Unless otherwise stated, scripture quotations are from the New Revised Standard Version Bible, copyright © 1989 by the Division of Christian Education of the National Council of the Churches of Christ in the U.S.A. Used by permission. All rights reserved.

Scripture quotations designated REB are from *The Revised English Bible* (a revision of The New English Bible) and © Oxford University Press and Cambridge University Press 1989. Reprinted with permission.

Scripture quotations designated KJV are from The King James Version of the Bible.

Cover design: Left Coast Design, Portland, OR
Cover photo: Scott Barrow Photography
Interior icon development: Michael C. McGuire, settingPace
Second printing: 2008

ISBN 978-0-8358-9830-0

Printed in the United States of America

For more information on *Companions in Christ*
call 800-972-0433 or visit www.companionsinchrist.org

Contents

Acknowledgments

Companions in Christ is truly the result of the efforts of a team of persons who shared a common vision. This team graciously contributed their knowledge and experience to develop a small-group resource that would creatively engage persons in a journey of spiritual growth and discovery. The authors of Part 1 were Rueben P. Job and Marjorie J. Thompson. Stephen Bryant was the primary author of the daily exercises and the Leader's Guide. Marjorie Thompson created the original design and participated in the editing of the entire resource. Keith Beasley-Topliffe served as a consultant in the creation of the process for the small-group meetings and contributed numerous ideas that influenced the final shape of the resource. In the early stages of development, two advisory groups read and responded to the initial drafts of material. The persons participating as members of those advisory groups were Jeannette Bakke, Avery Brooke, Thomas Parker, Helen Pearson Smith, Luther E. Smith Jr., Eradio Valverde Jr., Diane Luton Blum, Carol Bumbalough, Ruth Torri, and Mark Wilson. Prior to publication, test groups in the following churches used the material and provided helpful suggestions for improvement of the Participant's Book and the Leader's Guide.

First United Methodist Church, Hartselle, Alabama
St. George's Episcopal Church, Nashville, Tennessee

Acknowledgments

Northwest Presbyterian Church, Atlanta, Georgia
Garfield Memorial United Methodist Church,
    Pepper Pike, Ohio
First United Methodist Church, Corpus Christi, Texas
Malibu United Methodist Church, Malibu, California
First United Methodist Church, Santa Monica, California
St. Paul United Methodist Church, San Antonio, Texas
Trinity Presbyterian Church, Arvada, Colorado
First United Methodist Church, Franklin, Tennessee
La Trinidad United Methodist Church, San Antonio, Texas
Aldersgate United Methodist Church, Slidell, Louisiana

My deep gratitude goes to all these persons and groups for their contribution to and support of *Companions in Christ*.

—Janice T. Grana, editor of *Companions in Christ*
April 2001

Introduction

Welcome to Part 1 of *Companions in Christ*, a small-group resource for spiritual formation. It is designed to create a setting where you can respond to God's call to an ever-deepening communion and wholeness in Christ—as an individual, as a member of a small group, and as part of a congregation. The resource focuses on your experience of God and your discovery of spiritual practices that help you share more fully in the life of Christ. You will be exploring the potential of Christian community as an environment of grace and mutual guidance through the Spirit. You will grow closer to members of your small group as you seek together to know and respond to God's will. And your congregation will grow when you and your companions begin to bring what you learn into all areas of church life, from classes and meetings to worship and outreach.

How does *Companions in Christ* help you grow spiritually? It enables you to immerse yourself in "streams of living waters" through the spiritual disciplines of prayer, scripture, ministry, worship, study, and Christian conversation. These means of grace are the common ways in which Christ meets people, renews their faith, and deepens their life together in love.

• Through *Companions*, you will explore the depths of scripture, learn to listen to God through it, and allow your life to be shaped by the Word.

- Through *Companions*, you will experience new dimensions of prayer, try fresh ways of opening to God, and learn what it means to practice the presence of God.

- Through *Companions*, you will reflect on Christ's call in your life and discover anew the gifts that God is giving you for living out your personal ministry.

- Through *Companions*, you and members of your group will grow together as a Christian community and gain skills in learning how small groups in the church become settings for spiritual guidance.

Although *Companions* is not an introductory course in Christianity for new Christians, it will help church people take up the basic disciplines of faith in renewing and transforming ways.

An Outline of the Resource

Companions in Christ has two primary components: individual reading and daily exercises throughout the week with this Participant's Book and a weekly two-hour meeting based on suggestions in the Leader's Guide. For each week, the Participant's Book has a chapter introducing new material and five daily exercises to help you reflect on your life in light of the content of the chapter. After the Preparatory Meeting of your group, you will begin a weekly cycle as follows: On day 1 you will be asked to read the chapter and on days 2–6 to complete the five daily exercises (found at the end of the chapter reading). On day 7 you will meet with your group. The daily exercises aim to help you move from information (knowledge about) to experience (knowledge of). An important part of this process is keeping a personal notebook or journal where you record reflections, prayers, and questions for later review and for reference at the weekly group meeting. The time commitment for the daily exercises is about thirty minutes. The weekly meeting will include time for reflecting on the exercises of the past week, for moving deeper into learnings from chapter readings, for having group experiences of prayer, and for considering ways to share with the congregation what you have learned or experienced.

The complete material in *Companions in Christ* covers a period of twenty-eight weeks divided into five parts or units, of which this volume is the first. The five parts are as follows:

1. *Embracing the Journey: The Way of Christ* (five weeks)—a basic exploration of spiritual formation as a journey toward wholeness and holiness, individually and in community, through the grace of God.

2. *Feeding on the Word: The Mind of Christ* (five weeks)—an introduction to several ways of meditating on and praying with scripture.

3. *Deepening Our Prayer: The Heart of Christ* (six weeks)—a guided experience of various forms and styles of prayer.

4. *Responding to Our Call: The Work of Christ* (five weeks)—a presentation of vocation or call: giving ourselves to God in willing obedience and receiving the fruits and gifts of the Holy Spirit.

5. *Exploring Spiritual Guidance: The Spirit of Christ* (five weeks)—an overview of different ways of giving and receiving spiritual guidance, from one-on-one relationships, to spiritual growth groups, to guidance in congregational life as a whole.

Your group may want to take a short break between units either to allow for some unstructured reflection time or to avoid meeting near Christmas or Easter. However, the units are designed to be sequential—each unit builds on previous ones.

Your Participant's Book includes a section titled "Materials for Group Meetings." This section includes some brief supplemental readings that you will use as a part of several group meetings. Your leader will alert you when you will be using this material. Also you will find an annotated resource list that describes additional books related to the themes of various parts of *Companions in Christ*.

You will need to bring your Participant's Book, your Bible, and your personal notebook or journal to the weekly group meeting.

The Companions in Christ Network

An additional dimension of *Companions in Christ* is the Network. While you and your group are experiencing *Companions in Christ*, groups in other congregations will also be meeting. The Network provides opportunities for you to share your experiences with one another and to link in a variety of meaningful ways. As you move through the resource, there will be occasions when you will be invited to pray for another group, send greetings or encouragement, or receive their support for your group. Connecting in these ways will enrich your group's experience and the experience of those to whom you reach out.

The Network also provides a place to share conversation and information. The Companion's Web site, www.companionsinchrist.org, includes a discussion room where you can offer insights, voice questions, and respond to others in an ongoing process of shared learning. The site provides a list of other Companions groups and their geographical locations so that you can make connections as you feel led.

The Companions Network is a versatile and dynamic component of the larger *Companions* resource. A Network toll-free number (1-800-972-0433) is staffed during regular business hours to take your order.

Your Personal Notebook or Journal

"I began these pages for myself, in order to think out my own particular pattern of living.... And since I think best with a pencil in my hand, I started naturally to write." Anne Morrow Lindbergh began her beloved classic, *Gift from the Sea*, with these words. You may not imagine that you "think best with a pencil in hand," but there is something truly wonderful about what can happen when we reflect on the inner life through writing.

Keeping a journal or personal notebook (commonly called journaling) will be one of the most important dimensions of your personal experience with *Companions in Christ*. The Participant's Book gives you daily spiritual exercises every week. More often than not, you will be asked to note your thoughts, reflections, questions, feelings, or prayers in relation to the exercises.

Even if you are totally inexperienced in this kind of personal writing, you may find that it becomes second nature very quickly. Your thoughts may start to pour out of you, giving expression to an inner life that has never been released. If, on the other hand, you find the writing difficult or cumbersome, give yourself permission to try it in a new way. Because a journal is "for your eyes only," you may choose any style that suits you. You need not worry about making your words sound beautiful or about writing with good grammar and spelling. You don't even need to write complete sentences! Jotting down key ideas, insights, or musings is just fine. You might want to doodle while you think or sketch an image that comes to you. Make journaling fun and relaxed. No one will see what you write, and you have complete freedom to share with the group only what you choose of your reflections.

There are two important reasons for keeping a journal or personal notebook as you move through *Companions in Christ*. First, the process of writing down our thoughts clarifies them for us. They become more specific and concrete. Sometimes we really do not know what we think until we see our thoughts on paper, and often the process of writing itself generates new creative insight. Second, this personal record captures what we have been experiencing inwardly over time. Journaling helps us track changes in our thinking and growth of insight. Our memories are notoriously fragile and fleeting in this regard. Specific feelings or creative connections we may have had two weeks ago, or even three days ago, are hard to recall without a written record. Even though your journal cannot capture all that goes through your mind in a single reflection period, it will serve as a reminder. You will need to draw on these reminders during small-group meetings each week.

Begin by purchasing a book that you can use for this purpose. It can be as simple as a spiral-bound notebook or as fancy as a cloth-bound blank book. Some people prefer lined paper and some unlined. You will want, at minimum, something more permanent than a ring-binder or paper pad. The Upper Room has made available a companion journal for this resource that you can purchase if you so desire.

When you begin the daily exercises, have your journal and pen or pencil at hand. You need not wait until you have finished reading and thinking an exercise through completely. Learn to stop and write as you go. Think on paper. Feel free to write anything that comes to you, even if it seems to be "off the topic." It may turn out to be more relevant or useful than you first think. If the process seems clumsy at first, don't fret. Like any spiritual practice, it gets easier over time, and its value becomes more apparent.

Here is how your weekly practice of journaling is shaped. On the first day after your group meeting, read the new chapter. Jot down your responses to the reading: "aha" moments, questions, points of disagreement, images, or any other reflections you wish to record. You may prefer to note these in the margins of the chapter. Over the next five days, you will do the exercises for the week, recording either general or specific responses as they are invited. On the day of the group meeting, it will be helpful to review what you have written through the week, perhaps marking portions you would like to share in the group. Bring your journal with you to meetings so that you can refer to it directly or refresh your memory of significant moments you want to paraphrase during discussion times. With time, you may indeed find that journaling helps you to think out your own pattern of living and that you will be able to see more clearly how God is at work in your life.

Your Group Meeting

The weekly group meeting is divided into four segments. First you will gather for a brief time of worship and prayer. This offers an opportunity to set aside the many concerns of the day and center on God's presence and guidance as you begin your group session.

The second section of the meeting is called "Sharing Insights." During this time you will be invited to talk about your experiences with the daily exercises. The group leader will participate as a member and share his or her responses as well. Generally the sharing by each member will be brief and related to specific exercises. This is an important time for your group to learn and practice what it means to be a community of persons seeking to listen to God and to live more faithfully as disciples of Christ. The group provides a supportive space to explore your listening, your spiritual practices, and how you are attempting to put those practices into daily life. Group members need not comment or offer advice to one another. Rather the group members help you, by their attentiveness and prayer, to pay attention to what has been happening in your particular response to the daily exercises. The group is not functioning as a traditional support group that offers suggestions or help to one another. Rather, the group members trust that the Holy Spirit is the guide and that they are called to help one another listen to that guidance.

The "Sharing Insights" time presents a unique opportunity to learn how God works differently in each of our lives. Our journeys, while varied, are enriched by others' experiences. We can hold one another in prayer, and we can honor each other's experience. Through this part of the meeting, you will see in fresh ways how God's activity may touch or address our lives in unexpected ways. The group will need to establish some ground rules to facilitate the sharing. For example, you may want to be clear that each person speak only about his or her own beliefs, feelings, and responses and that all group members have permission to share only what and when they are ready to share. Above all, the group needs to maintain confidentiality so that what is shared in the group stays in the group. This part of the group meeting will be much less meaningful if persons interrupt and try to comment on what is being said or try to "fix" what they see as a problem. The leader will close this part of the meeting by calling attention to any patterns or themes that seem to emerge from the group's sharing. These patterns may point to a word that God is offering to the group. Notice that the group leader functions both as a participant and as someone who aids the process by listening and summarizing the key insights that have surfaced.

The third segment of the group meeting is called "Deeper Explorations." This part of the meeting may expand on ideas contained in the week's chapter, offer practice in the spiritual disciplines introduced in the chapter or exercises, or give group members a chance to reflect on the implications of what they are learning for themselves and for their church. It offers a common learning experience for the group and a chance to go deeper in our understanding of how we can share more fully in the mind, heart, and work of Jesus Christ.

As it began, the group meeting ends with a brief time of worship, an ideal time for the group to share special requests for intercession that might come from the conversation and experience of the meeting or other prayer requests that arise naturally from the group.

The weeks that you participate in *Companions in Christ* will offer you the opportunity to focus on your relationship with Christ and to grow in your openness to God's presence and guidance. The unique aspect of this experience is that members of your small group, who are indeed your companions on the journey, will encourage your searching and learning. Those of us who have written and edited this resource offer our prayers that God will speak to you during these weeks and awaken you to enlarged possibilities of love and service in Christ's name. As we listen and explore together, we will surely meet our loving God who waits eagerly to guide us toward deeper maturity in Christ by the gracious working of the Holy Spirit.

Part 1

Embracing the Journey:
The Way of Christ

Rueben P. Job and
Marjorie J. Thompson

Part 1, Week 1
The Christian Life As Journey

I was six years old when my family took a trip of more than one day. We traveled from North Dakota to Wyoming—my parents, two brothers, and I, along with clothes and food for many days—all packed into a 1929 Durant automobile. My parents had planned carefully for overnight stops, and daily meals were served from an old wooden apple crate. We ate lunches beside the road or in a shady village park. Breakfast and supper were shared where we spent the night at roadside cabins that preceded modern motels.

It was a long journey filled with uncertainties. The car was not always dependable. Poorly marked and inadequately maintained roads resulted in a rough and dusty ride. Moreover, we had never traveled this way before. Our simple road map needed frequent interpretation, gleaned from truck drivers and other fellow travelers.

But what a glorious trip it was! Every day was filled with new surprises and sometimes with delight beyond description. The entire journey informed and transformed us as we shared new perceptions, made discoveries, and learned from our experience together.

We learned, for example, to be patient when the engine stopped and we had to wait for help. We learned that adversity could be encountered and overcome as we experienced one flat tire after another. We learned how to face the unexpected as road construction forced detours

to areas we had not planned to see. We discovered the simple joy of bread, fruit, and sausage, and the incomparable refreshment of cool water shared in the journey's pause. We marveled at vast prairies and the majesty of mountains seen for the first time. Our little car shook from a violent summer thunderstorm on the plains, and we trembled at the awesome power of nature.

After more than sixty years, memories of that journey remain vivid. My brothers and I still reflect on it when we get together. Lessons learned in that experience continue to inform my life, especially my spiritual life.

Movements in the Journey

I can well understand why Christian spirituality is often described as a journey rather than a destination. The spiritual life is characterized by movement and discovery, challenge and change, adversity and joy, uncertainty and fulfillment. It is also marked in a special way by companionship, first with the One we seek to follow and second with those who also seek to follow Jesus Christ.

The Bible is filled with images of spiritual life as journey. Perhaps the most remarkable illustration of spiritual journey in the Bible is the story of the Exodus. For forty years the Hebrew people struggled to move from Egyptian bondage to the freedom of the Promised Land. Some trials were met with obedience, others with dismal failures of faith, yet God's constant faithfulness kept them safe through the wilderness sojourn.

Hebrew Bible scholar Walter Brueggemann suggests that the life of faith is a journey with God characterized by three basic movements: (1) being oriented, (2) becoming disoriented, and (3) being surprisingly reoriented.[1] The psalms give consistent evidence of movement through such phases. I suspect these movements are familiar experiences to most of us who have embarked on an intentional spiritual journey. There are times when our certainties about life seem seriously undermined, if not completely shattered. There are other times when, through conscious effort or quite apart from it, we move

> *The Christian life involves more than growth and development. It involves conversion and transformation, a radical turning of the Self toward the God who made us and who continues to sustain us. Christian faith is about an inner transformation of consciousness resulting from our encounter with the living Christ.*
>
> —James C. Fenhagen

from disorientation to a new constellation of meaning and wholeness. Life is not a stationary experience. New insights and developments continually challenge our understanding of life and our experience of God. Yet if we see the spiritual life as a journey, these cycles of change will not alarm us or turn us aside from our primary goal—to know and love God.

The Journey of Jesus and His Followers

Jesus' life gives us a supreme example of spiritual life as journey. Like us, Jesus began his earthly sojourn as a helpless, vulnerable infant, completely dependent on the nurture of his parents and the providential grace of God. He grew from childhood to the maturity of adulthood, all the while coming to fuller consciousness of his identity in relation to the One he knew as Father. Even at age twelve, he was at home in his Father's house among the elders of Jerusalem. He was firmly "oriented" in his unique relationship with God and received divine affirmation for his vocation specifically in his baptism and at his transfiguration. Jesus knew intensely personal communion with God. He knew many high and holy moments of divine power manifested in and through himself; he knew the joy of community with his disciples and with the crowds who revered him. But he was not immune to struggle, disappointment, or the sting of rejection from friend and foe alike. Surely the experience of temptation in the wilderness was one of disorientation and reorientation for Jesus. On more than one occasion, Jesus expressed his frustration with disciples and others who repeatedly misunderstood his teachings and his basic purpose. Even more, the agony of Gethsemane, the experience of betrayal and denial by his closest human companions, and the ultimate horror of feeling abandoned even by God reveal a depth of disorientation in Jesus' life journey that defies our comprehension. Yet Jesus pioneered for us the ultimate reorientation to God's loving purpose in the glory of his resurrection. God's final word is life, not death; communion, not separation!

Jesus' journey is in some sense a model for each of his followers,

A spiritual life is simply a life in which all that we do comes from the centre, where we are anchored in God: a life soaked through and through by a sense of [divine] reality and claim, and self-given to the great movement of [God's] will.

—Evelyn Underhill

although each will experience the particular pattern of the journey in a different way. We have glimpses of that pattern for the twelve disciples who began their journey by accepting Jesus' call to follow him. Along with many days of wearying travel, punctuated by ridicule and rejection from some, came stunning moments of revelation and wonder: impossible healings, the miraculous feeding of the multitudes, the calming of a sudden storm on the lake. The disciples learned only gradually and imperfectly who Jesus was. Whatever certainties they had about him were thrown into crisis at their last Passover supper and in the devastation of the crucifixion. Yet beyond this profound disorientation came experiences of the risen Lord. One of the most powerful stories is the one of two disciples on the road to Emmaus. Here, two little-known men discovered the risen Christ as companion and teacher on their path of confusion and sorrow. The completely new orientation to life and meaning those disciples received remains a powerful promise for our own experience of life in faith.

The Nature of Our Journeys

Perhaps we have been fortunate enough to have been given a secure orientation to God's love early in life. Even so, we cannot long escape the disorienting blows life inevitably brings: the death of a loved one; flagrant injustice in the world or in our own lives; the sins of prejudice, greed, and power-grasping that result in so many evils. It is often difficult to perceive the reality of God's presence, much less the goodness of divine grace, in these profoundly disturbing experiences. Yet God's grace comes in more shapes than security in danger or comfort in the midst of painful disjunctures.

True devotion to God means seeking the divine will in all things. Over time, life teaches us that not getting what we want in prayer may be just what we need. It is part of God's gift that we are weaned away from false notions of who God is, as well as false understandings of what God wants us to be. To imagine that God is here simply to console, affirm, heal, and love us is to deny the holiness of a God who requires righteousness, who challenges our illusions, who con-

fronts our idolatries. When we are being "disillusioned" from false perspectives, the spiritual journey feels arduous—more like climbing a steep mountain than like driving the great plains. Indeed, at times it feels like going over the edge of a cliff on nothing but the thin rope of faith. Sometimes we are called to endure in hope when we can see nothing positive on the horizon at all.

Reorientation to a deeper, richer, and less brittle faith is the potential that lies within truly disorienting life experiences. But this gift does not always come as soon as we would wish or necessarily in the way we hope for. God's ways are profoundly mysterious to us. It is only by faith that we can claim boldly the promise of Romans 8:28: "We know that all things work together for good for those who love God, who are called according to his purpose."

The Promise of Our Faith

God is good and works continually for good in the world, especially in and for and through those who love God. However, the goodness of God's purposes in the world is not accomplished without suffering. We see this truth most clearly in the life of Jesus Christ. Jesus himself promises his followers that they too will suffer in this world if they choose to be his disciples. Yet the greater promise is joy, the incomparable joy of a life lived not for our own sake or from our own center, but for God and centered in Christ. Life in Christ is life abundant! It is possible to know this joy even in the midst of turmoil and suffering. The enduring practices of scriptural reflection, prayer, worship, and guidance within the community of faith help us discover and live these spiritual truths personally and corporately. Exploring such practices together is the purpose of this resource.

Throughout Jewish and Christian history, life with God—the spiritual life—has been seen as a journey. It will be natural, then, during the course of these weeks of reflection and formation to look at our own spiritual life this way. Each of us is on a journey personally, but we will also be covenanting to journey together for a time in the process of deeper exploration represented by this small-group experience. We can help one another remember that the spiritual life is not complete maturity but growth in Christ. We have not arrived but are moving toward God and, therefore, toward the fulfillment of our potential as children of God.

The writer of Ephesians calls us "to maturity, to the measure of the full stature of Christ" (4:13). Such maturity is connected to sound teaching, for it is characteristic of the spiritually immature to be susceptible to "every wind of doctrine" (v. 14). To "grow up in every way into him who is the head, into Christ" (v. 15), signifies a capacity for unity in Christ, an ability to show in our individual lives that we are part of a healthy, unified, life-giving organism called the church. When members of the church are properly equipped with God's truth in Christ, when each part of the whole works as it should, the church grows by "building itself up in love" (v. 16). And the more we build the church up in love, the more like our Lord we become. "What we will be has not yet been revealed. What we do know is this: when he is revealed, we will be like him" (1 John 3:2). This is the goal of the Christian life, a topic we will explore further in the next section.

In everything, keep trusting that God is with you, that God has given you companions on the journey.

—Henri J. M. Nouwen

DAILY EXERCISES

Be sure to read the first chapter, "The Christian Life As Journey," before you begin these exercises. Keep a journal or blank notebook beside you to record your thoughts, questions, prayers, and images. In preparation for each exercise, take a few moments to quiet yourself and let go of particular concerns from your day. Release yourself to God's care, and open your heart to the guidance of the Holy Spirit. In the exercises this week you will be given the opportunity to reflect on your experience of the spiritual life as a journey of faith.

EXERCISE 1

Read Genesis 12:1-9. This story is about an unsettling event in Abram's life that marked the beginning of the faith journey of the Hebrew people. What marked the beginning(s) of your faith journey—your conscious movement from the "land" you knew to the "land" that the Lord would show you? Write down your remembrances, reflections, and feelings about what got you started. Pause to share your feelings with God.

EXERCISE 2

Read Genesis 28:10-22. This story is about God's waking Jacob up to the divine presence and promise in his life. If you were able to walk back through your personal history, where would you marvel with Jacob, "Surely the Lord is in this place—and I did not know it"? Take a mental tour of your early, middle, and recent years, prayerfully repeating this phrase in connection with each memory. Jot down remembrances and any new awareness of God's presence. Close by expressing your gratitude to God.

EXERCISE 3

Read Exodus 17:1-7. This story tells of the Israelites' faith struggles as they "journeyed by stages" from slavery in Egypt through the wilderness. Identify a stage in your journey when you were spiritually thirsty, discouraged, or empty. What happened? What brought you through

the desert? Write your reflections. Close by sharing your questions and wonderings with God.

EXERCISE 4

Read Psalm 126. This psalm expresses the Israelites' joy upon returning home after years in exile. When have you experienced the joy of reunion with a person, place, or community of deep significance to you? When in your spiritual journey have you felt restored in your relationship with God? Record your reflections. Give thanks to God for always welcoming you home.

EXERCISE 5

Read Luke 24:13-35. This story is about two disciples who experienced rapid movements from being oriented (before Jesus' crucifixion) to being disoriented (vv. 13-24) to being reoriented (vv. 25-35). Their story mirrors our own as we grow in our walk with Christ. Which of these movements best describes where you find yourself right now? Record your insights. Spend a few minutes in prayerful conversation with Christ about where you perceive his presence or inward prompting in your life.

Remember to review your journal entries for the week in preparation for the group meeting.

The Nature of the Christian Spiritual Life

hat is the Christian spiritual life? It is simply life lived in Christ—that is, a life where Christ rather than our own self-image constitutes the center of who we are. It is a Spirit-filled, Spirit-led, Spirit-empowered life like the one Jesus embodied with every fiber of his being. Empty of self-importance and self-interest, human life is free to be what God intended: holy, humble, joyfully obedient, radiating the power of love. Paul describes this state of being succinctly in Galatians 2:20: "It is no longer I who live, but it is Christ who lives in me." This, at least, is what a mature Christian life looks like. Most of us feel quite acutely how far we fall short of such spiritual maturity. While it offers a beautiful vision of human capacity and a noble goal, it may seem a daunting, if not impossible, ideal.

That is why we need to begin with grace. The spiritual life is not even remotely possible for us apart from God's grace. And grace is precisely what God gives to us in Jesus Christ. We find some of the most helpful writing in all of scripture on the subject of grace in the letter to the Ephesians. This brief letter contains a treasure trove of truths to help us understand and live the Christian spiritual life. Indeed, many scholars count Ephesians as the "crown jewel" of the church's theology.

The accent on grace is present from the opening greeting: "Grace to you and peace from God our Father and the Lord Jesus Christ." But

We humans, who are a due part of your creation, long to praise you. . . . You arouse us so that praising you may bring us joy, because you have made us and drawn us to yourself, and our heart is unquiet until it rests in you.

—Augustine of Hippo

the full scope and content of grace become especially evident in chapter 1:3-14. I invite you to read this passage through now at a reflective pace before we continue.

The author of Ephesians[1] begins by blessing the God who has gifted us "with every spiritual blessing" in Christ. It is really quite awesome to think that God "chose us in Christ before the foundation of the world to be holy and blameless before him in love." The rich blessings that come with this gift are many: We are forgiven and redeemed from sin, adopted as children of God, given the inheritance of salvation and knowledge of the mystery of God's will. This is our destiny, chosen not by us but by God for us. And all this abundance of grace is a sheer expression of God's goodwill toward us in Christ. We are being drawn irresistibly to the purpose for which we were made: to praise God with joy!

The Book of Ephesians gives us here a sweeping and convincing portrait of God's tremendous goodwill toward us. It pictures a comprehensive plan for all creation, gathered up in Christ, the Word made flesh. The mystery of this plan is Christ's sacrificial love: Though we have fallen far from grace by sin, in him we are forgiven, reconciled, restored to holiness. God's greatest desire and good pleasure are to bless us in Christ Jesus! Nothing will be withheld from those who live in him by faith. The single word that sums up the central truth of this passage is *grace*.

Grace: An Illustration

Grace is one of those words that floats around in the vocabulary of religious conversation with little examination. No doubt each of us has had an experience of grace, and no single experience is defining for everyone. Grace is hard to define, yet we often recognize what it is by experience. The following illustration comes from a childhood memory. Perhaps it will help you to discover and name your own experiences that give meaning to the word *grace*.

Receiving a slingshot was a big event when I was a child. I remember well when my father made my first one. He cut the Y from a chokecherry tree and used rubber bands from an old truck inner tube, and leather from the tongue of a discarded shoe to hold the stone. When he finished, my father took a few practice shots with little pebbles and then handed the slingshot to me with some low-key but firm instructions about its use. He told me never to shoot at a window, animal, or bird, and never to aim at anything that I did not intend to break, injure, or kill.

It all started well. I was the happiest five-year-old in the county! Ammunition was without limit, and targets were everywhere. Trees, leaves, fence posts, rocks, and water puddles all received well-aimed stones from my slingshot.

One spring evening just after we had finished eating, I was out playing with my slingshot when a mourning dove caught my attention. I knew I was not supposed to shoot at the bird, but I also knew the chances of a "hit" were very, very small. So I pulled up the slingshot and let a stone fly in the direction of the dove. Much to my shock and dismay, the bird fluttered, wounded and helpless, to the ground. I was frightened and heartbroken because I did not want to anger or disobey my father.

I ran indoors and went straight to bed with my clothes on! Soon I heard my father enter the room, and the next thing I knew he was sitting on the side of my bed. He asked me why I was in bed; and through my tears, I blurted out the story of my failure to act responsibly with the slingshot he had made for me. He pulled me to himself and held me as I cried. We talked about the danger of breaking rules designed to keep us and all of God's creatures safe. In his arms I found forgiveness and the promise of another chance. Soon we were walking out the door hand in hand rehearsing what it meant to be a responsible owner of a slingshot.

Grace often comes in unexpected ways and unexpected places. However it comes, it is always unmerited, pure gift. We cannot earn it, purchase it, or even destroy it. The writer of Ephesians makes this clear in the second chapter: "For by grace you have been saved through faith, and this is not your own doing; it is the gift of God—not the result of works, so that no one may boast" (vv. 8-9).

Why would God choose to gift us so lavishly when all of us have been disobedient—sometimes willfully and sometimes unknowingly? As the letter explains, it is simply "so that in the ages to come [God] might show the immeasurable riches of his grace in kindness toward us in Christ Jesus" (Eph. 2:7). It is God's nature to love with overflowing kindness. Indeed, in a deeper sense, grace is the gift of God's own presence with us, "freely bestowed on us in the Beloved" (Eph. 1:6). Jesus is the Beloved, a name revealed in his baptism (Matt. 3:17). Every spiritual gift—love, purity, mercy, peace, truth, fidelity, simplicity, joy—is an offering of God's own nature to us in Christ Jesus. Such grace is given for our comfort, healing, guidance, and transformation. It is given so that we might have life in abundance.

The Goal of the Spiritual Life

Now we can return to the "impossible ideal" of the Christian life. It is by the grace of God in Christ that we are enabled, very gradually, to become what God has destined us to be.

We are destined to be conformed to the image of Christ, who is himself "the image of the invisible God" (Col. 1:15); the divine image in which we were originally created is restored to us in Jesus Christ. But this process of being reshaped according to God's intended pattern takes time. It is the work of the Holy Spirit and is called sanctification in Christian theology. After turning our hearts back to God and receiving the justification that comes through faith in Christ, then begins the work of bringing our whole character in line with that of Christ. We begin to mature in knowledge, wisdom, and love. Our growth in the Spirit is marked by movements up and down, forward and backward, and sometimes even in circles! For human beings, the spiritual life is no straight line of unimpeded progress. It is, however, by God's unwavering goodness, always undergirded by grace. This is what gives us the hope and courage to persevere. Persevering on the journey is illustrated quite simply by the response a monk once made to a curious person's question, "What do you do up there in that monastery anyway?" The monk replied, "We take a few steps,

Grace transforms our dreadful failing into plentiful and endless solace; and grace transforms our shameful falling into high and honourable rising; and grace transforms our sorrowful dying into holy, blessed life.

—Julian of Norwich

then we fall down. Then we get up, take another step, and fall down again. And then we get up. . . . " As someone has observed, "It is not falling in the water that drowns us, but staying there."

Precisely because God is so gracious and generous toward us, in the face of all our waywardness, the Christian life is especially marked by gratitude and trust. Gratitude is the hallmark of the heart that knows its Redeemer personally and intimately. Grasping the true significance of God's gift overwhelms the soul with thanksgiving. And a thankful life is naturally a generous life, desiring ways to give something back to God, however small the gesture may seem.

The grace of God also teaches us to trust God's goodness and power. Only divine love is strong enough to transform the most unlovely of us into companions of our living Lord. Grace enables our cynical, burned-out spirits to see life with new eyes—eyes fresh with wonder like a child's. We continue to see evil, sin, and pain in the world. In fact, we see these things more clearly and feel them more acutely. But we see them encompassed by God's presence, purpose, and greater power of love. When we begin to see with the eyes of faith, we can accept God's power to heal, redeem, and transform each of us personally and all of us together.

The letter of Ephesians describes Paul's prison circumstances in this light. The apostle knew firsthand the suffering of persecution. He is portrayed writing this letter as "an ambassador in chains" (6:20), imprisoned for his faith yet feeling only deep affection and gratitude for the church, desiring above all that his new Christian flock might know the hope and inheritance to which it was called. Paul knew that God's power is made perfect in our weakness (2 Cor. 12:9) and that new life is unleashed through the suffering of crucifixion. It would be perfectly consistent for him to pray that the Ephesians would come to know "what is the immeasurable greatness of [God's] power for us who believe" (1:19).

Certainly the Apostle Paul knew from experience God's power to bring life out of death. His experience of the risen Lord turned him from persecutor to proclaimer of Christ. He perceived that his life as a Pharisee, "righteous under the law," was a form of spiritual death.

He knew the taste of life in Christ, the spiritual freedom of one who had received "grace upon grace." He saw that since he did not have to earn salvation by good works, he could give himself joyfully to good works as an offering of gratitude.

A Life of Continued Conversion

In essence, the writer of Ephesians comprehends the spiritual life as a life of conversion—conversion from falsehood to truth, from bondage to liberty, from death to life. Moreover, it is not just a one-time conversion, although Paul himself had a profound and specific conversion experience on the road to Damascus. The Christian life is one of continual conversion, daily turning from the old way of life to the new way we have come to know in Christ. That is why the writer urges the Ephesian converts to "lead a life worthy of the calling to which you have been called, with all humility and gentleness, with patience, bearing with one another in love, making every effort to maintain the unity of the Spirit in the bond of peace" (4:1-3).

Conversion is part of the process of maturing toward the full stature of Christ. The Ephesians have already received grace so that they no longer follow "the course of this world" (2:2). But they still need reminders not to "live as the Gentiles live" in greed and impurity. They need to hear about speaking truth to one another, working honestly, and using words to build one another up. "Put away from you all bitterness and wrath and anger and wrangling and slander, together with all malice," he says (4:31). This is not what they have learned of Christ! "You were taught to put away your former way of life, your old self . . . and to clothe yourselves with the new self, created according to the likeness of God in true righteousness and holiness" (4:20-24). What does the new life look like but to "be kind to one another, tenderhearted, forgiving one another, as God in Christ has forgiven you" (4:32)?

Like the Ephesians, we are "in process" in our faith. We have already received grace in more ways than we can name or even be aware of. Yet we also need to be reminded regularly of what a Christian life

The adventure with God is not a destination but a journey. The never-ending journey begins when you open the door and invite the Presence to come into your consciousness in an abiding way. Beginning the journey is like a wedding that takes places at a definable time; but the journey itself is like a marriage—it takes time to know and understand each other.

—Ben Campbell Johnson

looks and acts like. It takes practice to become "imitators of God." It takes freedom from self-interest to "live in love, as Christ loved us and gave himself up for us" (5:1-2). We need a great deal of support, encouragement, and practice in "clothing ourselves with the new self." Seeking God's continued grace for our practice is critical. But this is also where we discover that the community of faith is crucial to our sanctification.

The New Community

We cannot travel this path into new life alone, and we are not expected to. The risen Christ, who promised to be with us "to the end of the age," travels with us. But often it is through his body, the church, that we experience his presence with us most powerfully. We do not always experience the church this way, but it is undoubtedly what Jesus calls the church to be: a filling out of his presence in the world through the work of the Holy Spirit.

Ephesians makes it clear that the spiritual life is life in community as members of the body of Christ. It must be so because such life in community expresses the reconciliation and peace Christ died to give to us. Please read Ephesians 2:11-22 in connection with this discussion. The writer of Ephesians wishes the reader to understand that Paul, a Jew, is speaking here to Greek Gentiles. The cultural divide between Jews and Gentiles in his day was enormous, scarcely to be bridged by the best imagination or goodwill. While commerce might occur between them in a civil way, Jews perceived no connection with Gentiles at the level of religion. Gentiles had no part in the covenant promise. Yet Paul clearly preaches that in Jesus Christ, the wall of hostility and division between them has been dissolved. In his own body, Jesus has reconciled the two peoples into one, "that he might create in himself one new humanity" reconciled to one another and to God.

The community of faith in Jesus Christ is now the temple where God dwells: "In him the whole structure is joined together and grows into a holy temple in the Lord; in whom you also are built together spiritually into a dwelling place for God" (2:21-22). Indeed, the gifts

No one can develop a mature spirituality alone. To be a Christian is to be called into community. It is to become a functioning part of the body of Christ.

—Steve Harper

of the Spirit are given to individual members of the body only to build up the strength, integrity, and witness of the church. Gifts are "to equip the saints for the work of ministry, for building up the body of Christ, until all of us come to the unity of the faith and of the knowledge of the Son of God" (4:11-13).

The Christian spiritual life cannot be lived apart from community. Elizabeth O'Connor writes, "This is the most creative and difficult work to which any of us will ever be called. There is no higher achievement in all the world than to be a person in community, and this is the call of every Christian."[2] It is in the various communities of the church (including our families) that we should be able to share love, forgiveness, reconciliation, and a unity of spirit deeper than our surface differences. Naturally, we do not always experience these things in our congregations or families. Sin continues to have its hold on us, and it is hard to see that the victory of love has already been won. Yet the church is called to be the very community where we learn to live out the love of Christ in spite of and through our conflicts. We need to allow Christ to be our peace and to find our unity in him, since we will never achieve unity through our opinions!

Our task, ultimately, is to practice living the Christian life wherever we are. To enable this practice God gives us the great gift of grace. But we begin by receiving particular means of grace from the church to help us understand and live our faith. Historically these have included hearing God's Word preached and receiving the sacraments. The means of grace extend to praying in community, serving one another in humble love, receiving mutual guidance, and learning to discern the movement of the Spirit together.

The adventure upon which we are embarked in this course of experiential learning, as a small community of faith within the church, will help us begin to explore some of these means of grace both personally and corporately.

DAILY EXERCISES

Read the second chapter, "The Nature of the Christian Spiritual Life," before you begin these exercises. Keep your journal at hand to record reflections. Remember to quiet yourself, release your concerns to God, and open both mind and heart to the work of the Spirit. During this week, you will be reading from the Book of Ephesians and reflecting on the gift of God's grace in your life.

EXERCISE 1

Read Ephesians 1:1-14. The opening of this letter is like a downpour of blessing. Pay attention to the expressions of praise and prayer, allowing the many spiritual blessings with which God has blessed us to soak into the soil of your mind and heart. Which aspects of what God has done for us in Christ are most important for you? Reflect in your journal. Note any aspects that remain a mystery for you. Take time to offer your praise to God and to list other ways God has blessed and sustained you with grace.

EXERCISE 2

Read Ephesians 2:11-22. In your world of family, friends, church, or community, where is there a "dividing wall" with "hostility between us"? Offer the situation to God in prayer. Imagine Christ standing in peace between you and the one with whom you're in conflict, opening a way to live together in love. Write or draw what you see and feel about the gift Christ gives. What difference could it make, and what action does it call for on your part?

EXERCISE 3

Read the prayer in Ephesians 3:14-19 several times slowly as a way of internalizing its promise for you. First, read it as a prayer for you personally. Then pray it as a prayer for your family; next, as a prayer for your church; finally, as a prayer for the whole human family. After each reading, reflect in your journal on how the prayer opens your way

of seeing God's transforming grace in you. Take to memory a favorite phrase and carry it prayerfully in your heart throughout the day.

EXERCISE 4

Read Ephesians 5:6-20. These verses describe what it means to emerge from darkness and "live as children of light." As you read, reflect on where you find yourself saying "yes," "no," or "yes, but" to the counsel of these verses. In your journal, record a letter to the writer of Ephesians. Describe what you are learning about living as a child of light in our time and about the challenges for which we need guidance today. Read what have you written and see if God is speaking to you through your own words.

EXERCISE 5

Read Ephesians 6:10-17. To "take up the whole armor of God, so that you may be able . . . to stand firm" means to remain "rooted and grounded in love" (3:17). What inner and outer forces routinely uproot your faith, sap your inner strength, or undermine your courage to "stand firm" in Christ's love? What personal and communal practices nourish your roots in love and strengthen the life of God in you? What "armor" do you need to "take up"? Who can assist you in standing firm?

Remember to review your journal entries for the week in preparation for the group meeting.

The Flow and the Means of Grace

As we have said, the Christian life is possible only by the grace of God. Every awakening to God within us is the result of the Holy Spirit's action in and upon us. We are awakened to God and sustained in God by the initiative that the Holy One takes toward us and on our behalf. Just as life is pure gift, unrequested and beyond our power, so the spiritual life is offered to us from the heart of God long before we ever think of our walk with Christ.

The letter to the Ephesians proclaims that God's grace was flowing out to us before the foundation of the world. At the very beginning of creation we were chosen in Christ to live in love and peace with God (Eph. 1:4). God's grace precedes, follows, surrounds, and sustains us always. It is a constant and completely consistent gift. We cannot stop, alter, or change it. We are eternally cradled in God's abundant and life-giving grace.

While the initiative and the invitation to companionship are entirely God's, response lies with us. God gives us grace to respond to the awakening call of the Holy Spirit, but we can choose to turn away and refuse the invitation. Or we can choose, by the Spirit's help, to walk in faithfulness and harmony with God. By doing so we claim our true and full inheritance as children of God. Choosing to open ourselves to grace means receiving life's greatest gift and walking the path of spiritual abundance.

> *God's grace is not divided into bits and pieces, . . . but grace takes us up completely into God's favor for the sake of Christ, our intercessor and mediator, so that the gifts [of the Spirit] may begin their work in us.*
>
> —Martin Luther

This week we will explore further the nature of grace, the flow of grace, and the means of grace. How do we receive this gift for our redemption, joy, and fruitfulness as disciples? In what ways does grace shape and mold our lives as we move from being strangers to intimate companions of God?

The Nature of Grace

In my first year of school, I contracted scarlet fever. I became very ill and did not return to school for an entire year. For weeks I was delirious and unable to be out of bed. Then when I became strong enough to sit up, my mother prepared a special place for me to get well. We lived in a modified sod house with walls nearly three feet thick. Each window had a large, boxlike well inside the house, where my mother often kept plants through the winter.

When I was strong enough to sit up, my mother made a little nest of pillows for me in a south-facing window well. Then she carried me from my bed to this place of healing comfort. Perhaps she intuited the healing virtues of sunlight. Certainly, she knew I would be safe, warm, and near to her. While the illness was long and in many ways devastating, one of my happiest childhood memories is being nestled there in the light and warmth of the sun. I could look outside and see my father working. I could see and hear my mother nearby, cooking, mending, and doing what mothers of growing families did.

The winter sunlight, pouring through that south window, warming, giving light and hastening my healing, is for me a wonderful image of God's grace. The gift of grace is always present to give light, warmth, comfort, and healing.

The Christian concept of grace is rooted in scripture and always reflects God's redemptive love reaching out to us. The Bible tells the story of God's saving work on behalf of all people. This work is always undeserved, an expression of God's unconditional love for humankind. God offers love, redemption, covenant community, and companionship to each and all of us without precondition.

Christians see grace most clearly in God's act of self-giving through

The music of divine love plays uniquely in each person's life. Through individual personalities and personal life events, the goodness of God takes on a melody all its own. The song of God needs an instrument to give it shape and voice. ...We are all called to be instruments through which the melody of God takes shape. Through our lives God's love seeks to dance and make music for the world.

—Joyce Rupp

the person of Jesus Christ. In the suffering love and forgiveness of the cross, we perceive grace in all its fullness. Faith in Christ becomes the way we discover and apprehend this incredible gift (Rom. 5:1-2). From the beginning of creation we were meant to know ourselves as God's children, enjoying all of the benefits of our full inheritance (Eph. 1:5). Having lost our native inheritance through sin, we now receive these benefits through Jesus Christ. God's love and favor in Christ bestow them upon us.

The Flow of Grace

Our experience of grace represents a certain natural progression in the Christian life. Initially divine grace surrounds us without our conscious knowledge. We are simply immersed in God's unconditional, ever-present love. God works to protect us from spiritual danger and "woos" us in the unconscious infancy of our faith, calling us to be aware of grace. Once we have become fully conscious of a faith decision and choose to receive God's forgiving love in Jesus Christ, we experience the grace of justification. At this point the experience of grace helps us know that we belong not to ourselves but to our faithful Savior, Jesus Christ. We understand that righteousness before God is not something we earn; it can be received only as gift. As the Spirit builds on the foundation of justification, we gradually grow in holiness of life, or sanctification. This experience of grace leads us to bear the fruits of the Spirit and to exercise the gifts of the Spirit.

Creation is shot through with the self-gift of God. The divine life, the divine self-giving called grace, is the secret dynamism at the heart of creation.
—Maria Boulding

In one great strand of historic Christianity (the Wesleyan/Methodist), these experiences of grace have been called prevenient (or preceding) grace, justifying grace, and sanctifying grace. They are understood to represent a certain "flow" or progression from our introduction to God's grace to our completion in it. We move from unawareness toward intentional cooperation with God that enables us to accept our justification and grow into Christian maturity. According to John Wesley, the fruit of justifying grace is the "blessed assurance" of belonging to Christ; and the fruit of sanctifying grace is growth in holiness and perfection in love.

However, progression from one expression of grace to another is not automatic or as methodical as it may sound. Many areas overlap throughout our lives. God's pervasive and persuasive grace always upholds us. And God is continually at work to help us accept fully the gift of our justification, as well as to shape us into the perfect design for which we were created. Thus various expressions of grace operate at the same time, yet it is always one and the same love spilling out eternally from the heart of God, sweeping over us even when we are unable to appreciate or receive God's activity on our behalf.

Divine grace continues to draw us from death toward life, to provide the healing and cleansing of forgiveness and restoration, and to offer the strength and courage to move toward a more perfect life. We may receive these spiritual gifts through the means of grace.

The Means of Grace

Recalling how my mother placed me in the sunny window well so I could recuperate from deadly illness helps me make sense of the means of grace. Placing ourselves in a position where we may benefit most from the life-giving light of God's love is the purpose of every means of grace. The means of grace are methods and practices we use to "put ourselves in God's way." They help us adopt a posture of receptivity.

Although we cannot manipulate or control what God will give us through various means of grace, we can trust that grace will be given and that what we receive will be tailored to our specific situation. For instance, we may be "caught" by a passage of scripture today that we have read for years without ever being challenged, nurtured, or formed by it. Suddenly a certain text or story comes alive for us, and we will never be the same.

Grace comes to us in many ways as we make our journey Godward. While the ways are countless, certain means of grace have been practiced almost universally in the history of the church. Some are as old as humankind. Even if many or all are known to you, they require disciplined practice to make them your own.

The traditional means of grace include worship, the sacraments of baptism and the Lord's Supper, prayer, fasting, scripture reading,

and community. Each is a well-tested means to receive and appropriate God's life-giving grace. The means of grace have no merit in themselves, but they can lead us toward wholeness and deeper communion with God.

Worship

Corporate worship is an essential means of grace for any serious traveler on the Christian way. Worship has been identified as humankind's most profound activity. Nothing that we can do equals the act of worship in significance for us, the world about us, or the God before whom we come to offer worship. To gather with others who seek God's will and way is in itself a marvelous way of placing ourselves in a position to receive grace.

Protestants generally affirm the two sacraments of baptism and the Lord's Supper as means of grace. In baptism we recognize that God's active love on our behalf precedes our birth and surrounds us eternally. The psalms declare that we would not exist were it not for God's grace (Pss. 119:73; 139:13). In the covenant of baptism we accept our adoption as God's children by grace and promise our faithful response. We are incorporated into the body of Christ and become a part of the church, the covenant community of faith (1 Cor. 12–13).

For most Christians, the Eucharist, or Lord's Supper, is the central act of worship. There we declare who God is and who we are in God's presence. At the table of the Lord all are needy and hungry; all are invited to come for healing and sustenance. No believer is turned aside; all equally receive God's unmerited forgiveness, peace, and presence. Our unity in humility with our Lord, who emptied himself in sacrificial love for us, spiritually unites us with one another in this meal. The grace of communion with Christ is simultaneously a grace of communion with one another in the fellowship of faith.

Prayer

Prayer is often recognized as the most central and profound means of grace. Prayer is native language to all of us, young and old, of every

The sure and general rule for all who groan for the salvation of God is this,—whenever opportunity serves, use all the means [of grace] which God has ordained; for who knows in which God will meet thee with the grace that bringeth salvation?

—John Wesley

race and creed. Prayer is a language we learn as we explore the mystery of life, often prompted by gratitude that craves expression or by pain that cries for relief. It is a language learned through questions without answers and life-giving discoveries that arise over the course of our journeys. It is a language learned while searching for guidance on the way and in response to direction clearly given.

While we may never have formally decided to pray or may forsake the way of prayer for a time, most of us have some experience with this means of grace. For many people, prayer is as natural as breathing; for others, it requires intense effort and concentration. For some, prayer is joyful companionship with Jesus Christ; for others, it is a struggle to keep the relationship with God vital. Some nurture their relationship with God through prayerful living; others are so consumed with living that they have little time or energy left for prayer. Regardless of our situation, prayer remains a primary means of grace.

A loving, living relationship with God is impossible without prayer. We cannot know the mind and heart of Christ, receive God's direction, hear God's voice, or respond to God's call without this means of grace. We may enter God's kingdom without the benefit of some of the means of grace but not without prayer. Prayer is so important that Jesus left even the needy crowd to pray (Mark 6:31). His entire life and ministry were set in the context of prayer. Those who choose to follow him can do no better than to take up his example.

The disciple on an intentional spiritual journey will discover prayer to be an indispensable means of nurturing intimacy and companionship with the living Christ. A classic writer of Christian spirituality once noted that prayer is the mortar that holds our life together. Prayer is really not so much about us as it is about God. Prayer is simply our response to the invitation of grace to come home and live with God all the days of our lives, in this world and the next.

Richard Foster lists twenty-one kinds of prayer! Others identify fewer types. The number of forms is less important than the faithful practice of whatever form you are led to. Those who have gone before us in faith have left much wise counsel on how to pray. The third part of this resource will look at prayer in more depth as a means of grace.

Fasting

Dallas Willard identifies fasting as a spiritual discipline of abstinence.[1] From ancient times onward, fasting has been understood as a practice that opens our lives to receive God's gifts. Fasting has had two primary purposes for those seeking to walk with God: first, repentance; and second, preparation to receive God's strength for faithful living.[2] Fasting has often been connected with prayer to form a powerful way of receiving the gifts of grace.

Fasting suggests a laying aside of our personal appetites, desires, and even felt needs in order to hear more clearly the call of God. It is a way of emptying our hands and our lives so that they may be filled with God. Food, entertainment, sex, possessions, activity—all good gifts in their time and place—can be focused upon to the exclusion of God. You might ask yourself what now fills your life to the point of crowding God out. The answer will likely lead you to the kind of fast that could be a special means of grace for you.

When beginning to fast for the first time, you do well to move slowly. Try a short fast to see how you respond. If you have physical problems, it is best to seek medical advice when fasting from food.

A fast can be made more meaningful if it is shared with another person or a praying community. It is important that each person in the group agree on the purpose of the fast and to the kind of fast being undertaken. Take time to discuss these matters. After such decisions have been made, you will be ready to move on to the details, such as duration and starting and ending times.

Many contemporary Christians report fasting to be a wonderful means of grace that brings clarity and direction to the spiritual life. Some people fast one day a week; others, for special occasions only. You will want to pray for guidance when you consider fasting as a means of grace for yourself and those with whom you journey.

Scripture

Next to prayer, scripture reading is the most profound means of grace for most persons on an intentional spiritual journey. To read and to meditate upon the scriptures every day raises our awareness of God's presence in our lives in remarkable ways. The transforming experience of living daily with scripture will, over the course of a lifetime, shape our hearts and minds more and more into the image of Christ.

Scripture records God's mighty acts, including creation and God's ongoing relationship with humankind. It is a record of God's self-revelation. For Christians, this revelation finds its apex in the Incarnation when God chose to become flesh in the person of Jesus of Nazareth. Some have said that God has given us three books of revelation: nature, history, and the Bible. Most Christians would probably agree that the Bible speaks most clearly of God's person and purpose. The second part of this resource will focus directly on the spiritually formative power of the Bible.

Other Considerations

The community of faith is also a means of grace. Since the entire fifth week of Part 1 is devoted to Christian community as a means of grace, it is mentioned here only to note its importance.

Sometimes we speak of the means of grace as spiritual disciplines. The word *discipline* may have harsh connotations for us. True spiritual disciplines are never externally imposed. Rather, they are "practices that help us consciously to develop the spiritual dimensions of our lives. Like an artist who wishes to develop painting skills, or an athlete who desires a strong and flexible body for the game, a person of faith freely chooses to adopt certain life patterns, habits, and commitments in order to grow spiritually."[3]

Spiritual disciplines are practices that have proven to be effective in opening the windows of our lives to the refreshing, life-giving breath of God. There are many spiritual practices, but none has merit in itself. The value lies in one simple test: how effectively the disciplines turn our lives toward God and open our hearts to the Holy Spirit. Countless faithful witnesses to Christ assure us that we may trust the Spirit to guide us to those means of grace that will be most transforming for us. May we have the faith and courage to follow.

DAILY EXERCISES

Read the third chapter, "The Flow and the Means of Grace." Keep your journal at hand to record your reflections. Remember to take time for silence, turn your attention to God, and open yourself to the guidance of the Holy Spirit before each exercise. This week's exercises will guide you to reflect on the movements of grace in your life and the means by which God has touched you.

EXERCISE 1

Read Luke 15:11-32. Jesus tells a parable about the loving father of two sons. With which of the sons do you identify, and how? Reflect on how the younger son "came to himself." When have you come to yourself, recognized your need, and begun a return to God? How have you experienced the seeking love of God's prevenient grace?

EXERCISE 2

Read Luke 15:11-32 again. Jesus' parable portrays a forgiving father who is foolishly in love with his two sons. Reflect on the father's response to his younger son's return, even "while he was still far off." When have you experienced such compassion, acceptance, and forgiveness (whether you were far from God in a way more like that of the younger or the elder son)? How did you respond? How have you experienced the saving love of God's justifying grace?

EXERCISE 3

Read Luke 15:11-32 again. Jesus seems to have told the parable primarily to address the "elder brother" tendencies in the Pharisees and in us, confronting our smallness of heart. How do you think you would have responded to the return of the younger son? Where do you believe that you are growing in your ability to love and forgive, and where do you still feel blocked? In other words, where are you experiencing the call and challenge of God's sanctifying grace?

EXERCISE 4

Read Luke 15:11-32 once more. Jesus' parable is full of actions that serve as outward and visible signs of each character's inward and spiritual condition. Go back and note each action of the father as an outward means of expressing the inward grace of his welcoming heart, his readiness to forgive and fully restore the son's wasted life. Through what means of grace (traditional or nontraditional) has God touched you, restored you, and encouraged your growth? Reflect on your baptism as a means by which God runs to us while we are "still far off" to embrace and kiss us and to clothe us in newness. Reflect on your experience of Holy Communion as a means by which God continues to celebrate our movement from death to life.

EXERCISE 5

Read Luke 15:11-32 a final time. Look at Jesus' parable as an unfinished story about a family on a journey of healing and wholeness. Use your imagination to continue the story from the perspective of one of the three characters or as an imaginary observer, such as a neighbor watching through a window. For instance, what does the father say to the younger son the day after the party about what it means to be back in the family? Does the elder son remain resentful, or does the father's love prevail in transforming his attitude? Do the sons grow to share the life and love of their father? How does your way of completing the story reveal your assumptions about God, people, and yourself?

Remember to review your journal entries for the week in preparation for the group meeting.

Sharing Journeys of Faith

We began this small-group study with some reflections on the image of journey as a metaphor for life and growth in faith. A younger generation apparently has tired of hearing the term *journey* applied to human emotional and spiritual maturation; yet it remains a remarkably apt metaphor. In a very deep sense, life is pilgrimage. Its earthly expression moves from a beginning to a distinct destination. It traverses a great deal of terrain psychologically, intellectually, and physically. There are certain markers on the journey, common stages we go through in the process of development. But there are also unique experiences that mark our individuality, sometimes in indelible ways. The timing of one's particular life path is always deeply personal, directed by many forces beyond one's control—family, circumstances, environment, location in history and place—as well as by the choices one makes in relation to these forces.

It helps to recognize, at least to some extent, the character and contours of the spiritual journey. When we see some of the main routes and major turning points along the life-path, we may begin to articulate their meaning for us and, if we choose, to share that meaning with others on the path.

A helpful way to become more conscious of the shape of the spiritual path over time is to look at the lives of some great and faithful

Powerful stories throughout history . . . teach us what it means to be a follower of Jesus. Our own life stories and the stories of our communities of faith serve as icons that help to shape our ways of being and doing.

—Dwight W. Vogel and
Linda J. Vogel

forebears in the faith. What motivated their search for God? How might we characterize their spiritual journeys? What were some significant turning points, and how did they interpret the meaning of these for themselves?

Models of the Faith Journey

Perhaps Augustine of Hippo (354–430 C.E.) was the first to write a true spiritual autobiography. His *Confessions* is a remarkable testament to searching self-examination, and it remains engaging reading for Christians sixteen centuries later! Augustine had a formidable intellect, so it is not surprising that his quest for God took the form of an intellectual search for truth. While his writing is filled with passion, deep feeling, and spiritual depth, it is the sheer power of his mind to penetrate, analyze, and describe the character of his inner life that is so impressive. For a man of a "prepsychological age," Augustine had an astute capacity to diagnose his own mind and heart in a way that astonishes modern readers.

Augustine's personal obsession with finding truth led him through several philosophies popular in his day. But gradually, his mind led him away from the doctrines of the Manichees and Neoplatonists. He complained that the Manichean orators continually talked about truth, "although the truth was nowhere to be found in them." Addressing God directly, as he does throughout the *Confessions*, Augustine exclaimed, "Truth, truth: how in my inmost being the very marrow of my mind sighed for you!"[1] In the very next paragraph he acknowledges, "But my hunger and thirst were not even for the greatest of your works, but for you, my God, because you are Truth itself *with whom there can be no change, no swerving from your course* (James 1:17)."[2] Although not capturing all the complexity of Augustine's journey, it would be fair to say that his path to God was one of intense inquiry, a path through the gift of the mind.

Martin Luther, twelve centuries later, embodies another kind of journey. Luther, who was (ironically) part of an Augustinian order as a young man, was driven by a different need in his search for God.

Possessed of a vibrant, expansive, tempestuous personality and an agonized conscience, Luther felt inwardly that he could never be sure of his salvation. A common maxim of his time was "Do that which is in you to do, and leave the rest to God." Even though the maxim was intended as a counsel of comfort to help overly scrupulous monks find release from self-imposed efforts to win divine grace, Luther felt he could never be sure that he had done all that was in him to do! What was meant as a word of grace was, for him, an impossible demand and a heavy weight of judgment. The need to be righteous before God was like an albatross around his neck.

The deep issue for Luther was that while he knew of God's grace intellectually, he could not assimilate it emotionally. Young Martin grew up as a child of medieval German lore. Influenced by old beliefs in capricious water sprites and malevolent forest spirits, he harbored something of a terrorized soul. Here are his own words from the Preface to his *Latin Writings*: "Though I lived as a monk without reproach, I felt that I was a sinner before God with an extremely disturbed conscience. I could not believe that he was placated by my satisfaction. I did not love, yes, I hated the righteous God who punishes sinners, and secretly . . . I was angry with God." [3]

Interestingly, both Augustine and Luther had conversion experiences that were connected to passages in Paul's letter to the Romans. For Luther, the passage was Romans 1:17, in particular the phrase, "The one who is righteous will live by faith." The dawning recognition that righteousness is a gift we receive simply by faith was, for Luther, an enormous release from the emotional burden of believing that he was somehow required to fulfill what he considered an impossible expectation. Listen again to his own words: "I felt that I was altogether born again and had entered paradise itself through open gates. . . . And I extolled my sweetest word with a love as great as the hatred with which I had before hated the word 'righteousness of God.'" [4]

Luther's spiritual journey was not so much a quest for intellectual truth as a quest for heartfelt assurance of God's grace. It was the path of an anxious heart in search of comfort. Not infrequently, a fearful or deeply wounded heart impels us toward God.

We see quite another kind of journey in the life of Mother Teresa of Calcutta, a beloved saint of our own era. She had the capacity to see Christ in the faces of the poor. Born to Albanian parents who named her Agnes, the woman later known as Mother Teresa had no great intellect or any apparent deep emotional need. Agnes was a simple and rather unpromising nun in the eyes of some of her superiors. But she felt deeply called to a very focused task: that of caring for the poorest of the poor—the sick and dying of Calcutta's ghettos who were despised and forgotten by everyone else. Mother Teresa had a vision of giving herself to Christ by loving each person created in God's image, no matter how unloved or unlovely: "Whoever the poorest of the poor are, they are Christ for us—Christ under the guise of human suffering."[5] Her mission was not to save as many as possible or to change social structures. It was to love one person at a time— each a beautiful soul, a child of God, a person of unique and irreplaceable value to God. "I feel called to serve individuals, to love each human being. My calling is not to judge institutions. . . . If I thought in terms of crowds, I would never begin my work. I believe in the personal touch of one to one."[6]

Mother Teresa and the Missionaries of Charity she founded were driven Godward by a hunger for holiness expressed in relationships of service to the needy, what John Wesley called "social holiness." It is a path to God marked by active love. While rooted in worship and contemplation, this journey is neither primarily intellectual nor emotional but essentially physical. With the body one lifts and soothes and touches the sorely wounded of the world. Here is a path to God through the gift of the physical being.

Still a different kind of journey is represented in the life and ministry of Evelyn Underhill, another spiritual giant of the modern era. Widely read during the first half of the twentieth century, her prolific writings on the spiritual life are a relatively unknown treasure of Christendom today. Evelyn was born in England and raised in the Anglican Church. By the early 1920s, this brilliant woman was earning a reputation as an expert in the field of mystical theology, yet her own spiritual life felt to her like an intolerable burden of loneliness and isolation. She could not find herself fully at home either in the Church of England or in the Roman Catholic Church. Sharing her prayer life with no one, Evelyn was "cut off from sacramental life and the possibility of community that might have sustained her."[7]

A major turning point came with Evelyn's first retreat at an Anglican retreat house called Pleshey. There in the quiet beauty of the Essex countryside, Evelyn began to experience a sense of being at home in the church of her birth for the first time. She wrote to her spiritual director Baron von Hügel, "The whole house seems soaked in love and prayer. To my surprise a regimen of daily communion and four services a day with silence between was the most easy unstrained and natural life I had ever lived."[8] Interestingly enough, this retreat had the effect not of leading her into further withdrawal from others but of curing her solitude: "I lost there my last bit of separateness. . . . My old religious life now looks . . . thin and solitary."[9]

It was not long before Underhill began conducting spiritual life retreats for others at Pleshey. A gifted spiritual guide and retreat leader, she gave more than a decade of her life to this ministry for which she is as much beloved as for her many books. She understood from experience that a true retreat reconnects us with our living Source, so that we find ourselves more truly connected with one another. Time spent in worship, silence, and communion refreshes our spirits at a depth no other activity can match.

Evelyn's path to God was marked by hunger for union with Reality (her favorite name for God). She journeyed home by way of contemplation. Contemplation is essentially the wordless path to union with God. Yet her life was filled with writing, lecturing, and active service to the homeless in her community. Just as Mother Teresa's path was primarily active but rooted in contemplation, Evelyn's was primarily contemplative but expressed in a balance of activities. Like the journey of Teresa of Avila or Thomas Merton, Evelyn Underhill's journey was a remarkable blend of action and contemplation. A mystic at heart, she championed the path of interior quiet and listening.

Finding Connections

To oversimplify the matter, these four figures represent in turn a primary path to God through mind, heart, body, and spirit. Many other persons of faith could illustrate these basic pathways just as well. These particular figures are offered to help "prime the pump" for thinking about your own spiritual path. Do you tend to approach God by struggling with theological issues and intellectual questions? Through conflicted feelings and deep wounds? With a compelling desire to love others in simple service? Through the yearning for inward peace and a sense of being at home in a spiritual tradition? Is there some other path you would identify as your own?

God draws each one of us to the heart of life in a time and manner uniquely suited to our own nature and circumstance. Your journey and mine cannot be the same, even if we are identical twins! Yet our many journeys share remarkable commonalities, points where we find comfort in human identification and common ground. The signs of God's grace at work in us are often strikingly similar: perhaps a sense of being overwhelmed by prayer answered beyond our best hopes; the experience of anguish over prayer not answered the way we had hoped, yet in retrospect answered in an unexpected and perhaps deeper way; the intuition that God has called us to a task we felt was beyond our gifts or capacity, yet through faith and perseverance, we discovered it to be a genuine call for which God equipped us.

I hope these suggestions have whetted your appetite for looking at your own spiritual journey more closely. Where or how did you start out? Who most influenced your spiritual growth? When did you discover a new sense of direction, and where did it take you? What major experiences have shaped your journey, and how? These are just a few of the questions that can help you attend to the course of your spiritual development.

It is absolutely crucial . . . to keep in constant touch with what is going on in your own life's story and to pay close attention to what is going on in the stories of others' lives. If God is present anywhere, it is in those stories that God is present.

—Frederick Buechner

Telling Your Story

One way to observe and tell your faith journey is to write a simple spiritual autobiography. It need not be as profound or comprehensive as Augustine's *Confessions*, but it should be as honest and clear-sighted as you can make it. Such a document would be for your eyes only. Begin with your earliest memories of anything related to your faith, and carry the story forward to the present. Note the influence of your religious tradition or lack of it, your family's way of relating to faith, and mentors and peers along the way. Pay attention to the deep motivations behind your searching and finding. Look at the balance between your need for solitude and your desire for community, the inward aspects of your faith and their outward expressions. Describe your experience of prayer. Notice the significant turns, conversions, and changes along the way. See if you can identify a "primary path" in your story.

You might also choose to draw your spiritual journey. Take a large sheet of blank paper, or tape several together for adequate space. Draw a line that represents your life, showing the ups and downs, turns, circles, or whatever pattern seems right to you. Mark particularly significant events with symbols that represent what they have meant in your faith life. Be creative with this process, using colors to express your feelings at various times or gluing onto the paper other materials that expand and interpret your symbols.

You may prefer to write a poem or a series of poems that give voice to the more interior and intangible aspects of your spiritual life. See if you can identify several experiences or circumstances that have been keys to your spiritual path in life. They might be things such as a significant move in childhood; a traumatic, challenging, or inspiring time in adolescence or young adulthood; the loss of a deep relationship; a change of career direction; an experience of another culture. Allow the feelings, images, and metaphors connected with the experience to surface in your reflection. Write a poem about each one that expresses for you the spiritual dimension of that experience. Often our experience of God does not lend itself to descriptive prose writing. Art, music, dance, and poetry are the language of the soul.

Remembering our stories helps us perceive ways God has shared in our personal history. We remember incredible answers to prayers and grace moments, times when God helped us through what seemed impossible crises.

—Richard Morgan

DAILY EXERCISES

Read the fourth chapter, "Sharing Journeys of Faith," before beginning these exercises. Keep a journal of your reflections. Settle yourself in openness and expectancy before God as you begin each one. These exercises will help us consider various models of the faith journey and prepare us to articulate our own spiritual stories.

EXERCISE 1

Read Galatians 1:11–2:1. We see that Paul's transformation in Christ was not immediate but took place over time. In time, he received a revelation of Christ, went apart to seek understanding, conferred with the other apostles, and worked out his calling in community.

Review the section called "Models of the Faith Journey." With which person described do you most identify? Why? What affinity or resistance do you feel toward each of the four persons? Share your feelings with God and listen. Can you name another "model of faith" with whom you particularly identify? Why? Note your reflections.

EXERCISE 2

Read Mark 12:28-30. Jesus reaffirms that the first commandment is to "love the Lord your God" with your whole being—heart, soul, mind, and strength. Which of these four aspects represents your primary path to God? For example, has your search for a deeper relationship with God been more related to your heart (affection and hunger for love), soul (intuition and desire for union with God), mind (inquiry and search for truth), or strength (action and serving the common good)? Which motivation is strongest? weakest? Has your motivation or manner of searching changed over the course of your journey? Capture your reflections in your notebook.

EXERCISE 3

Read Psalm 116. Complete verse 1 for yourself: "I love the Lord, because. . . . " Write your own expression of what connects you with

God and what God has done for you. Then take a few minutes to read back through your written reflections on the exercises from the first three weeks. Try to name the pivotal moments in your spiritual history, chapters in your story, and even a title for your unfinished story. What would be the name of the chapter you are now writing for God? Give thanks to God for the uniqueness of your journey.

EXERCISE 4

Read Psalm 107. This psalm, like many other psalms, tells faith stories of people. Were you to add to this psalm a stanza for your story, how would it read? Spend some time today and tomorrow thinking about the various ways you might describe or tell your spiritual life story. Choose a way that suits you to portray, express, or picture your story. For example, you might "draw" your journey, using an image or metaphor that captures the uniqueness of your spiritual history. You might write a poem or a brief autobiography that tells of formative influences and experiences. You could sketch a graph of high and low moments, diagram the paths you have followed, draw a "tree" of the people through whom God has shaped you, or make a collage of significant images. Be creative; let the Spirit guide you. Take these two days to work on your spiritual life story. Then be prepared to share your journey with the group in whatever way is comfortable for you. You will have ten to fifteen minutes to share whatever you choose about your story.

EXERCISE 5

Read Psalm 136. Spend a few minutes giving thanks for the steadfast love of God in your life and all the ways you have experienced it. Finish the work you began yesterday. Invite the Spirit into your efforts!

Remember to review your journal entries for the week in preparation for the group meeting.

Living As Covenant Community

*L*ife-threatening situations often reveal the character of people involved in them. My first adult bout with life-threatening illness revealed as much about the character of those around me as it did about my own. The first person to offer support, outside of family, was a member of the covenant group that I had been part of for more than a decade. While I was struggling to stay conscious, I knew that along with my family my covenant group had thrown a cloak of love and prayer around me. At this critical time, when I had great difficulty with rational thought or prayer, trusted colleagues were praying for and with me. To know that I was held in the light of God's presence by the prayers of God's faithful servants gave me great peace and comfort. The unqualified support of those in covenant relationship with us is but one important benefit of community. There are many more; some are hinted at in the following paragraphs, and others can be discovered only as you explore the richness of living in mutual covenant with others.

Christians are called into a community of mutual servanthood, and covenant groups are an ideal place to live out this calling. Each of us has a unique gift to offer to others. Small communities of covenant commitment are places where we can share and strengthen our gifts. In this group we discover our need for acceptance, growth, and accountability; here we may also see that need met.

We were not created to live in isolation. . . . While no one questions the need for periods of solitude and refreshment in our lives, faith tends to thrive most readily when shared and experienced with others.

—Mary Lou Redding

Tilden H. Edwards says that community is "what everyone wants but almost no one is able to sustain well for long."[1] Edwards is right. To form a genuine community takes intentional and committed effort. That is precisely what a covenant represents. Covenant community does not happen by accident. To sustain such community requires consistent attention and commitment. Perhaps that is why there are so few of us in long-standing covenant communities today. We may not know how to begin such a community, and we are often reluctant to pay the price of time and effort to sustain it.

But we do yearn for the benefits of covenant community, for meaningful relationships with others who intentionally set their faces and life journeys toward God. It is lonely to be serious about the spiritual life in our time. Those who are aware of their hunger for a deeper life with God often feel isolated and misunderstood. We need others to help us see and hear ourselves clearly. We need others to explore with us the edges of our fear and faith. We grow spiritually only in and through our relationship with God and with others.

We know that Jesus' life revealed a vital balance of solitude and community, the kind of wholeness and balance that we yearn to experience in our own lives. The twelve disciples became a trusted and beloved community, even though it was made up of persons like us with less than perfect understanding or character. Jesus valued community, finding both time and occasion to cultivate personal relationships with those who were his followers and closest friends (John 15:15). He also valued solitude, finding time and place to cultivate his inner life and relationship with God. Jesus was whole, with precisely the balance and rhythm of life we so desire for ourselves.

But how do we begin? Where do we look for such community? Who will companion us, and will we be compatible? Will we have the courage to form a community built on shared covenant? Can such a community be sustained in our culture? Do I personally have the capacity to live in covenant with others? What will it cost, and what are the rewards of covenant living? These are some of the questions that will undoubtedly come to us as we think about our participation in more intimate Christian community.

Biblical and Theological Roots of Covenant

When we explore the concept of covenant, we may think first of the covenants God fashioned with Abraham and Moses. Yet we can trace the origins of covenant as a defining element in God's relationship with us right back to Adam and Eve. From the beginning of creation, God has desired to be in a relationship of mutual love and accountability with humankind. God loves us with an everlasting love, expressed in abundant provision, protection, and divine companionship; we respond in love through gratitude and delight in God's goodness. God calls us to fidelity and creativity; we respond in obedience, seeking to join our hands and heart with the divine will.

Christian faith declares that God still desires and initiates covenant relationship with humankind today. As Christians, we begin our discussion of covenant community with the God who has been made known to us in Jesus Christ (Heb. 1:1-4). If we want to know what God intends for human life, we look at the life of Jesus. If we wish to know how God desires to shape us, we look to the contours of Jesus' life. Clearly Jesus lived out the depths of covenant relationship with God and with others.

Many theologians point to the mutual indwelling love of the three persons of the Trinity as a model of God's intention for us to live with God and one another in a communion of love. Since we are made in the divine image, we are already imprinted with the need, desire, and capacity for such communion. Biblical spirituality knows no such thing as private spirituality. It knows intimately personal relationship with God through inward solitude, but even in solitude we do not approach God in splendid isolation! The very first words of the Lord's Prayer declare our incorporation into community. When we offer this prayer, we recognize that we are part of God's larger family. Indeed, it is the unity Jesus knows with the Father and the Holy Spirit that he desires to give to all who follow him (John 17:20-23).

The church, described as the body of Christ, is by nature one vast community of covenant love (1 Cor. 12:12). From the moment of our baptism we are joined to a community of faith—local, global,

The more genuine and the deeper our community becomes, the more will everything else between us recede, the more clearly and purely will Jesus Christ and his work become the one and only thing that is vital between us. We have one another only through Christ.

—Dietrich Bonhoeffer

and cosmic—for this time and for all time. When we take vows of membership in the body of Christ, we intentionally place ourselves within a covenant community. We agree publicly to fulfill the obligations of covenanted life within the church. To unite with the church is to place ourselves within the circle of those who have sought, since the revelation of God in Christ, to love and obey God through being disciples of the risen Lord.

Marriage is a particular expression of Christian community based on mutual covenant that is often used to illustrate the shape and texture of covenant community. The covenant of marriage is fashioned as two people pledge their entire lives to each other. It is a covenant based on mutual love, trust, and commitment. For Christians, accountability in marriage is grounded in a larger community and in the presence of God.

From these illustrations we see some of the basic elements of Christian community. Of course, faith in God is the foundation for all else. Ultimately, it is God, through the power and action of the Holy Spirit, who forms us into community. No theologian has spoken this truth so clearly as Dietrich Bonhoeffer, who wrote, "Christian brotherhood is not an ideal which we must realize; it is rather a reality created by God in Christ in which we may participate."[2]

While our efforts are required, the fact remains that genuine community is a gift of God's marvelous grace. So we offer ourselves without reserve to God and permit our lives, at the direction of the Holy Spirit, to be built into covenant community. In this community we join others in seeking to be fully alive to God's presence each day.

Forms and Elements of Covenant Groups

Covenant groups in the church take various forms. In some, the content of group time is a particular study resource or spiritual practice. In others, the content of group time focuses on holding one another accountable to disciplines practiced individually outside of group time. The latter approach is sometimes called an accountable discipleship group.

In the first approach, group members may gather with a commitment to explore their faith over time by using books, tapes, videos, or other resources to generate thoughtful discussion and prayer. Some groups meet with a specific covenant to offer intercessory prayer, to practice Christian meditation, or to engage in contemplation together. Others meet to search scripture for guidance in daily life, perhaps using a group process of spiritual reading (such as that described in Part 2). Still others may commit to engage individually or together in active service to their wider communities, followed by group reflection and prayer.

Despite the variety of forms, the common elements in covenant groups generally include the following:

- Meeting together at regular intervals and faithfully attending meetings.
- Praying for the group as a whole and for each member.
- Sharing life and faith openly, in both light and dark sides of experience.
- Supporting, nurturing, and encouraging one another in Christian love.
- In a spirit of love, holding one another accountable to commitments made.
- Honoring the confidentiality of what is shared in meeting times.
- Joining together in some common outreach or form of ministry.

An absolutely essential element of Christian community that is seldom discussed is a willingness to offer to others one's true self rather than one's contrived self. The greatest gift we can give to another is the authentic self. One skilled leader has said, "A number of things take place in a community of grace. Perhaps the most prominent is that we become able to admit our secrets to others without fearing that they will reject us, and they become able to admit their secrets to us without fearing that we will reject them."[3] Here is how one woman

expressed this dynamic in her small group: "The groups became a place where you didn't have to pretend you had everything together as a person. You could just come and say, 'Here I am. This is the part of me that hurts. I need your help. I need to understand what God wants me to do in this case.' And so we got to talking about the real issues."[4] Only an atmosphere of genuine care, prayer, and confidentiality can build sufficient trust to encourage such honesty among group members.

We have already made some basic commitments as part of being in this group. However, we can learn much about our participation in this small group by exploring the benefits, rewards, and cost of life together. In this way we can look realistically at the meaning and reality of covenant community. In order to formulate a mutually supportive covenant we need shared goals. It is important to take time at the beginning of group formation to fashion a covenant that all find acceptable.

Willingness to give up personal choices for the sake of the larger community is probably one of the great hurdles for Christians who seek genuine community. Yet those who must always have their own way or who think they know best will consistently frustrate and impede the group development. These individuals will require deep conversion before they can participate fruitfully in any covenant community. In this matter Paul's words to the Philippians (2:3-4) are especially apt: "Do nothing from selfish ambition or conceit, but in humility regard others better than yourselves. Let each of you look not to your own interests, but to the interests of others."

Another key ingredient of covenant community often left unspoken and unexplored is the subject of mutual accountability. Holding one another accountable to commitments made can be an uncomfortable part of group life, especially in a culture that champions individualism and autonomous decisions. Most of us are wary of giving anyone else permission to hold us accountable for our choices and actions. We fear authoritarianism and self-righteous judgment. Only if we trust our sisters and brothers in Christ to love us unconditionally and desire to be accountable to them for at least certain aspects

When groups form to participate on a regular basis in spiritual practices, they frequently develop a deep bond. This bond is built not primarily by group-building practices but on the trust that develops when persons share the profound movement of God's work in their lives.

—Joseph D. Driskill

of our life in faith will we be able to accept this dimension of Christian community. Again, it is important that any group seeking to fashion a working covenant take the time to explore the meaning and benefit of accountability, feelings about it, and how it will be practiced in the group.

Naturally, an element in every search for community is the desire to experience the joy of mutual caring, sharing, and discovery in the Christian journey. When Christians form a covenant community, they have every right to expect unparalleled support and acceptance. But such support and acceptance do not happen automatically. Early discussion and planning can prompt each member to be alert to opportunities for care and ministry to one another.

Weighing Costs and Benefits

Now, what of the cost? Is covenant community worth the price? In our society we have become such bargain hunters that we are reluctant to "buy in" to anything that may ask too much and offer too little. A careful analysis of cost and benefit is a worthy endeavor. Saints who have traveled the path of life in community before us encourage us to count the cost and encourage us as well with report of the rewards. The cost includes relinquishing some portion of our autonomy, giving up a false and contrived self, giving our time, practicing a cultivated and careful listening, and being willing to do the hard work of holding one another close and accountable in love.

What are the benefits? Those who have journeyed on ahead of us would answer, "A taste of heaven." They are joined by the voices of many today who have experienced firsthand the fruits of covenant community. One participant in a women's group described the people she had come to love with a simple sentence: "They are like an extended family, one that you don't have to keep explaining yourself to over and over again."[5] Another man who felt constructively challenged by his group described the benefits this way: "The group makes me uncomfortable every week because I'm being challenged to give a little more and grow a little more and become a little more honest

with myself and a little more intimate with God or other people. And that's what I need very much."[6]

Entrusting oneself—body and soul—into the care of a loving, faithful community is one of the most rewarding and blessed experiences possible. To know that there is a praying, listening community ready to help me discern God's will and way in every eventuality of life offers me great assurance. To be reminded that every day my life is held close to the loving heart of God by those who seek only God's best for me is a wonderful gift. And to have the protection of a community that has the courage and faith to offer correction when I stray or a helping hand when I stumble is pure gift. Simply knowing that this caring and committed community stands with me, holds me, cares for me, and will not let me fall is enormous security and blessing in a world where such gifts are rare.

Morton Kelsey says, "Walking with others on their spiritual pilgrimages is an art."[7] How might each of us become an artist helping to create the beautiful mosaic of a living, growing, and life-giving community? Great artists have many native skills, but their work is the result of disciplined effort and a willingness to try and try again. Each of us has the capacity to live in covenant with other children of God. And each of us has native gifts to foster faithful living within the community. However, just as the artist constantly works at employing native gifts, so we constantly invest our skills and gifts in the effort to create community that more and more reflects the divine image.

Take courage and explore the meaning of covenant community with those sent by God to discover with you a fuller and richer discipleship than you have ever known. Remember, God calls, gathers, and forms every faithful community. This awareness alone gives us hope and courage to go on.

God has called us into being as a community and our life as a community, though fraught with struggles and failures, is a powerful act of revelation, testimony, and service.

—Rule of the
Society of St. John
the Evangelist

DAILY EXERCISES

Read the fifth chapter titled "Living As Covenant Community," keep your journal handy, and open yourself to God's spirit as you begin each exercise. The exercises this week are in preparation for discerning a group covenant at your next meeting. You are already part of a covenant group, since you have committed to the readings, daily exercises, and weekly meetings of *Companions in Christ*. This is just one more step in clarifying the type of small-group experience that you are seeking and what practices you would choose to support this community.

EXERCISE 1

Read Mark 3:13-19. The Twelve appointed by Jesus gathered around him in community, not simply to get to know one another, but to respond to a common call and a promise of shared life in God's kingdom. Take time to listen deeply to your heart now. What call do you hear, and what promise do you sense in being part of this group? What would you like to see the group become as you continue to journey together in Christ? Offer your hopes in all honesty to God. Capture significant thoughts, insights, and questions in your journal.

EXERCISE 2

Read Luke 22:21-34. This passage offers evidence both of joy and conflict in the community of disciples that Jesus called together. In his book *The Active Life*, Parker Palmer observes that one of the purposes of community is to "disillusion" us; that is, to dispel our illusions about God, others, and ourselves so as to bring us closer to the joy of truth. How have you experienced both joy and struggle as part of this group so far? Have you experienced disillusionment? If so, listen to what God may be saying to you through it. Write your thoughts.

EXERCISE 3

Read Philippians 2:1-4. Paul's counsel to "look . . . to the interests of others" calls us to a larger sense of who we are and, at the same time, challenges our grip on personal autonomy. Get in touch with your feelings of attraction and resistance to a covenant by which you agree to live in light of others' interests. Try to name what you like about that covenant and what you fear. Listen to what the Spirit may be saying to you about your feelings. Remember to capture your thoughts in writing.

EXERCISE 4

Read Psalm 133. Reflect on the relationship between the joy of community expressed in this psalm and the Hebrew context for community—covenant with God and one another. What in your experience are the agreements and practices needed for human community to be "good and pleasant" and a foretaste of God's "blessing, life forevermore"? What agreements and practices are needed for your small group to grow as a community in which everyone can persevere in grace and truth?

EXERCISE 5

Read Mark 6:30. Support and accountability both for the outward and the inward aspects of the spiritual journey were integral parts of the disciples' community with Jesus. What kind of support for practices, decisions, or changes would you welcome from this group? What kind of support would you resist? What kind of support would you be willing to offer others in the group? Prayerfully imagine yourself giving and receiving positive support in the group. What does such mutual support look like? Write your thoughts.

Remember to review your journal entries for the week in preparation for the group meeting.

Materials for Group Meetings

A Few Hymns Categorized by Faces of Grace

PREVENIENT

Come, Sinners, to the Gospel Feast

Come, Ye Sinners, Poor and Needy

I Sought the Lord

Tú Has Venido a la Orilla (Lord, You Have Come to the Lakeshore)

Softly and Tenderly

Pass Me Not, O Gentle Savior

Only Trust Him (Come, Every Soul By Sin Oppressed)

Blow Ye the Trumpet, Blow

I Surrender All

Spirit Song

Turn Your Eyes Upon Jesus

It's Me, It's Me, O Lord (Standing in the Need of Prayer)

Pues Si Vivimos (When We Are Living)

Alas! And Did My Savior Bleed

JUSTIFYING

Rock of Ages

And Can It Be

The Solid Rock (My Hope Is Built)

Blessed Assurance

I Stand Amazed in the Presence

Nothing Between

There Is a Balm in Gilead

It Is Well with My Soul

Just as I Am

A Mighty Fortress

Beneath the Cross of Jesus

Because He Lives

Grace Greater than Our Sin

He Touched Me

Victory in Jesus

Dona Nobis Pacem

Amazing Grace

SANCTIFYING

Love Divine, All Loves Excelling

Spirit of the Living God

Let There Be Peace on Earth

Jesu, Jesu

Be Thou My Vision

Trust and Obey

Have Thine Own Way, Lord

Come and Dwell in Me

This Is a Day of New Beginnings

Something Beautiful

Spirit of the Living God

Take Time to Be Holy

Seek Ye First

We Are Climbing Jacob's Ladder

Make Me a Captive, Lord

Breathe on Me, Breath of God

For the Healing of the Nations

The Voice of God Is Calling

An Annotated Resource List
from Upper Room Ministries

*T*he following books relate to and expand on the subject matter of the first volume of *Companions in Christ.* As you read and share with your small group, you may find some material that particularly challenges or helps you. If you wish to pursue individual reading on your own or if your small group wishes to follow up with additional resources, this list may be useful. The Upper Room is the publisher of the books listed, and the number in parentheses is the order number.

1. *A Wakeful Faith: Spiritual Practice in the Real World* (#912) by J. Marshall Jenkins. Jenkins assists us in recognizing ways the kingdom of God is flourishing in our midst and helps us to rouse and to deepen our hunger for God. With a biblical grounding, the author examines the spiritual dimensions of alertness to God. This book provides practical applications of spiritual wakefulness in daily living by showing how Jesus trained disciples to perceive the kingdom and to know God.

2. *Workbook on Becoming Alive in Christ* (#542) by Maxie Dunnam presents material for daily reflection, along with material for group discussion, on the subject of the indwelling Christ as the shaping power of our lives as Christians. This seven-week small-group resource will deepen your understanding of the Christian life and what it means to mature in Christ. Dunnam believes that spiritual formation requires discipline and practiced effort to recognize, to cultivate an awareness of, and to give expression to the indwelling Christ.

3. *Devotional Life in the Wesleyan Tradition* (#740) by Steve Harper explores the nature of the spiritual journey and Christian growth as seen in the writings of John Wesley. The author writes about the disciplines of prayer, scripture, the Lord's Supper, fasting, and Christian community. For Wesley, these disciplines are the means of receiving

God's grace in our lives. The workbook has sections for you to reflect upon and record your responses to the material. This is an excellent resource on the significance of spiritual disciplines or means of grace.

4. *Remembering Your Story: A Guide to Spiritual Autobiography,* revised (#963) by Richard L. Morgan is a ten-week study in which participants are helped to remember significant moments in their lives and how God was present to them. It is a creative approach to discernment for the past, present, and future. The accompanying leader's guide is #797. This resource includes many suggestions about how to focus on your memories of important people and events and link those memories with the biblical story.

5. *Hungering for God: Selected Writings of Augustine* (#830) in Upper Room Spiritual Classics series. This compilation offers some of the most profound and moving writings of the fourth-century African Christian who vastly influenced the Christian church and Western culture. Included are excerpts from Augustine's *Confessions* and other writings.

6. *Remember Who You Are: Baptism, a Model for the Christian Life* (#399) by William H. Willimon contains one of the very best explanations of the sacrament of baptism and is written in a way that is easy to understand. But it offers much more. The author is interested in helping you to remember your own baptism and to discover a new vision for what it means to be a disciple of Christ. The book presents in a graphic way the fundamentals of the faith.

Continue your exploration of the Christian journey by using *Companions in Christ: Exploring the Way* with your small group.

Exploring the Way: An Introduction to the Spiritual Journey
By Marjorie J. Thompson and Stephen D. Bryant
Participant's Book (0-8358-9806-7)
Leader's Guide (0-8358-9807-5)

Exploring the Way introduces basic concepts in the Christian spiritual life, along with biblical texts that undergird them. Stories and illustrations in each chapter help these basic concepts connect with daily experience. The resource offers definitions of terms frequently used today to describe the spiritual journey. The resource teaches the basics of simple spiritual practices that can help sustain the journey—practices such as scriptural meditation, prayer, daily examen, listening, and simple journaling.

Notes

Week 1   The Christian Life As Journey

1. Walter Brueggemann, *Praying the Psalms* (Winona, Minn.: Saint Mary's Press, 1982), 16–24.

Week 2   The Nature of the Christian Spiritual Life

1. While the church has traditionally attributed the writing of this letter to the Apostle Paul, many reputable scholars attribute it to a strong, second-generation Pauline community.
2. Elizabeth O'Connor, *The New Community* (New York: Harper & Row, 1976), 58.

Week 3   The Flow and the Means of Grace

1. Dallas Willard, *The Spirit of the Disciplines* (San Francisco: HarperSanFrancisco, 1991), 158.
2. Marjorie Thompson, *Soul Feast* (Louisville, Ky.: Westminster John Knox Press, 2005), 75–76.
3. Ibid., 10.

Week 4   Sharing Journeys of Faith

1. Augustine, *Confessions* 3.6, trans. Henry Chadwick (New York: Oxford University Press, 1991), 41.
2. Augustine, *Confessions* 3.6, trans. R. S. Pine-Coffin (New York: Penguin Books, 1961), 61.
3. *Martin Luther: Selections from His Writings,* ed. John Dillenberger (Garden City, N.Y.: Anchor Books, 1961), 11.
4. Ibid., 11–12.
5. Mother Teresa, *Mother Teresa: In My Own Words,* comp. José Luis González-Balado (Liguori, Mo.: Liguori Publications, 1989), 24.
6. Ibid., 99.
7. Deborah Smith Douglas, "Evelyn Underhill at Pleshey," *Weavings: A Journal of the Christian Spiritual Life* 14 (January–February 1999): 19.
8. Ibid., 20.
9. Ibid.

Week 5   Living As Covenant Community

1. Tilden H. Edwards, *Living in the Presence* (San Francisco: Harper & Row, 1987), 61.
2. Dietrich Bonhoeffer, *Life Together,* trans. John W. Doberstein (New York: Harper & Row, 1954), 30.
3. Clifford Williams, *Singleness of Heart* (Grand Rapids, Mich.: William B. Eerdmans, 1994), 116.
4. Robert Wuthnow, ed., *"I Come Away Stronger": How Small Groups Are Shaping American Religion* (Grand Rapids, Mich.: William B. Eerdmans, 1994), 15.
5. Ibid., 105.
6. Ibid., 153.
7. Morton T. Kelsey, *Companions on the Inner Way* (New York: Crossroad, 1983), 8.

Sources and Authors
of Margin Quotations

Week 1   The Christian Life As Journey
James C. Fenhagen, *Invitation to Holiness* (San Francisco: Harper & Row, 1985), 10.

Evelyn Underhill, *The Spiritual Life* (New York: Harper & Row, n.d.), 36.

Henri J. M. Nouwen, *The Inner Voice of Love* (New York: Doubleday, 1996), 39.

Week 2   The Nature of the Christian Spiritual Life
Augustine, *Confessions*, trans. Maria Boulding (Hyde Park, N.Y.: New City Press, 1997), 39.

Julian of Norwich, *Showings*, trans. Edmund Colledge and James Walsh (New York: Paulist Press, 1978), 263.

Ben Campbell Johnson, *Calming the Restless Spirit* (Nashville, Tenn.: Upper Room Books, 1997), 50.

Steve Harper, *Devotional Life in the Wesleyan Tradition* (Nashville, Tenn.: The Upper Room, 1983), 54.

Week 3   The Flow and the Means of Grace
Martin Luther, *Preface to the Letter of St. Paul to the Romans*, trans. Andrew Thornton, 1983, (27 May 1999) <http://www.ccel.org/l/luther/romans/pref_romans.html> (7 July 2000).

Joyce Rupp, *May I Have This Dance?* (Notre Dame, Ind.: Ave Maria Press, 1992), 118.

Maria Boulding, *The Coming of God* (Collegeville, Minn.: The Liturgical Press, 1982), 2.

John Wesley, "The Means of Grace" in *The Works of John Wesley*, vol. 5 (Grand Rapids, Mich.: Zondervan Publishing House, n.d.), 189.

Week 4   Sharing Journeys of Faith
Dwight W. Vogel and Linda J. Vogel, *Sacramental Living* (Nashville, Tenn.: Upper Room Books, 1999), 52.

Frederick Buechner, *Whistling in the Dark* (San Francisco: Harper & Row, 1988), 104.

Richard L. Morgan, *Remembering Your Story* (Nashville, Tenn.: Upper Room Books, 1996), 21.

Week 5   Living As Covenant Community
Mary Lou Redding, "Meeting God in Community," *The Spiritual Formation Bible* NRSV (Grand Rapids, Mich.: Zondervan, 1999), 1498.

Dietrich Bonhoeffer, *Life Together* (New York: Harper & Row, 1954), 26.

Joseph D. Driskill, *Protestant Spiritual Exercises* (Harrisburg, Pa.: Morehouse, 1999), 74.

The Rule of the Society of St. John the Evangelist (Cambridge, Mass.: Cowley Publications, 1997), 8.

COMPANION SONG

Piano Accompaniment Score

Lyrics by Marjorie Thompson

Music by Dean McIntyre

Optional cut for short version: omit measures 19-34.

Companions in Christ
Part 1 Authors

Rueben P. Job is a retired United Methodist bishop and former editor/publisher of The Upper Room. His titles for Upper Room Books include *A Guide to Prayer for Ministers and Other Servants, A Guide to Prayer for All God's People, A Guide to Prayer for All Who Seek God, A Guide to Spiritual Discernment,* and *Spiritual Life in the Congregation.*

Marjorie J. Thompson is an ordained Presbyterian minister, spiritual director, retreat leader, and director of Pathways in Congregational Spirituality in Nashville, Tennessee. She is the author of *Family the Forming Center, Soul Feast,* and several volumes of the Companions in Christ series.

Journal